FACE TO FACE WITH
MANATEES

by Brian Skerry

NATIONAL
GEOGRAPHIC
WASHINGTON, D. C.

FACE TO FACE

At Crystal River National Wildlife Refuge in Florida, an adult manatee comes to the surface to breathe. Manatees breathe in through their nostrils and then close them tightly as they dive back under the water.

There is something magical about meeting an animal in the wild. As an underwater wildlife photographer, it's my job to get close to animals in the sea. In fact, I have to get close to my subjects because it's hard to get a clear picture through water. So I spend a lot of my time just waiting for those fleeting moments when an underwater creature comes near enough that I can capture a good picture of it. These are special moments, when the animal chooses to be with you.

CAN MOLARS MARCH?

▬ Manatees have only one kind of tooth—the molar. A molar is a large back tooth for grinding food.

▬ Manatees take in a lot of sand and other grit along with all the plants they eat. This causes their teeth to wear down.

▬ When the teeth wear down too much, they fall out.

▬ New molars grow at the back of the mouth. These new molars move forward to replace the old ones. That's why they're called "marching molars."

I spent several weeks photographing manatees in Florida, at places like Crystal River National Wildlife Refuge. The best time to find them was either early in the morning or late in the afternoon as they gathered near freshwater springs. Wearing a mask and snorkel, I would slowly move to a place where they could see me. Then I would wait.

Many of the animals ignored me. But every once in a while, a manatee came right up to me! Sometimes we would even swim side by side.

After a few weeks, my wife, Marcia, and daughters Caroline (age 4) and Katherine (age 11) came to visit, and we went to look for manatees together. We got up early the first morning, loaded our equipment into a small boat, and slowly headed down the Crystal River. It was January. The air was cold, and thick fog clung to the warmer river water like a heavy winter blanket. Pulling on our wet suits, snorkels, and masks, we slipped quietly into the waist-deep water.

With our heads under water, we watched and waited. Pretty soon, we saw dozens of manatees gliding over the sandy bottom. A few manatees even came over and nudged our legs. They didn't seem

interested in us. But as my daughter headed back to the boat, her mom shouted, "Katherine, there's a little manatee swimming right behind you!"

Katherine turned around. She was face to face with a young manatee. It was curious and wanted to play. They swam together gently, moving away from the shore. When Katherine stopped swimming, the calf turned around and came back to her. They swam together for about ten minutes. But for Katherine, those ten minutes will last a lifetime!

▲ *My daughter Katherine swims with a playful young manatee in the Crystal River. The manatee seemed to enjoy the interaction, and it even swam right up under her arm.*

7

MEET

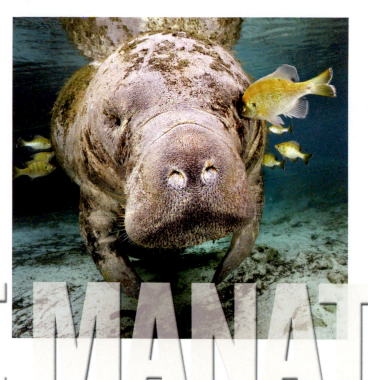

Some plants and animals make their home on the backs of manatees. Mats of algae often cover their rough skin. Fish eat the algae and the small animals that live in it.

THE MANATEE

Manatees use their flippers to steer through the water and to grip things, just like humans use their arms. Manatees even have tiny fingernails!

When early explorers sailed to the Americas, many of them reported seeing mermaids along the coast. Today, we know that they were probably looking at manatees. With its flippers that look like arms and the way it lifts its head above the water, a manatee does look a bit like a person with a fish's tail—from far away, at least. But once you've been face to face with a manatee, it's hard to believe that anyone could mistake one for a mermaid.

So what are manatees? They are mammals. Even

Spanish moss hangs from trees along the St. John's River, where manatees have gathered in the warm waters.

though they live their lives in the water, they are actually related to elephants. Like elephants, they have thick skin, sometimes more than 1 inch (2.5 cm) thick. Manatees don't have trunks, but they do have large flexible snouts that they use to grab and hold objects in the water. This is useful when feeding.

Like all other mammals, the manatee breathes air. It has two nostrils on the top of its snout. When the animal needs to take a breath, it pokes its snout out of the water and sucks in air through its nostrils. When a manatee is resting, it only comes to the surface to breathe every ten minutes or so. A manatee often floats just below the surface, taking a short breath with only its snout above the water.

Manatees grow 8 to 13 feet (2.4 to 4 m) long, and they can weigh up to 1,300 pounds (600 kg). Despite their large size, manatees are graceful swimmers. Their bodies are smooth and streamlined—ideal for underwater life. Manatees use their strong tails to push themselves through the water. But they usually move

▼ Manatees are often referred to as "sea cows." A group of them is called a herd. Males are called bulls, females are cows, and babies are called calves.

A manatee calf drinks milk, or nurses, from a gland behind its mother's flipper.

slowly. Manatees prefer water that is 3 to 15 feet (1 to 4 m) deep. In shallow water, they often use the tips of their flippers to walk along the bottom.

Manatees communicate with each other by making chirping squeaks and squeals. They also communicate by touch. They nuzzle each other and make contact with their flippers and tails.

Females usually give birth to one calf at a time. The mother helps the calf get to the surface to take its first breath. By the time the calf is one hour old, it swims alone. Newborn calves are about 4 feet (1.2 m) long and weigh 40 to 100 pounds (18 to 45 kg).

Like all mammal babies, a manatee calf nurses, or drinks milk, from its mother. When a calf is a few months old and still nursing, it will start to graze on water plants. Moms and calves form strong bonds. They stay together for up to two and a half years.

There are three kinds of manatees: West Indian, West African, and Amazonian. They all look and behave pretty much the same. The West

➡ *In Florida's Ellie Schiller Homosassa Springs Wildlife State Park, manatees are fed lettuce and other greens in a protected section of the river. The animals were brought here to recover after they had been injured.*

HOW DO MANATEES MUNCH AT LUNCH?

— Manatees eat a lot—up to 150 pounds (68 kg) of food a day.

— The snout, or upper lip, is very muscular and can grab plants.

— The bristles on the snout are like fingers and can tear off pieces of food and bring them to the mouth.

— Their flippers can hold the plants.

← In the United States, Florida is the best place to find manatees, in ocean waters as well as inland rivers and wetlands, such as the Everglades.

Indian manatee—the kind that my family and I met—ranges from Florida to Brazil.

In the warm summer months, West Indian manatees can be seen swimming along the coast from Florida to North Carolina. But when fall comes and the ocean temperature starts to drop, the manatees head back to Florida. They migrate into freshwater rivers and gather near natural springs, where the water is warmer.

Manatees are herbivores. They only eat plants—a lot of them! They spend 4 to 8 hours every day munching on sea grasses, water weeds, and algae. Every 24 hours, a manatee eats up to 1 pound (0.5 kg) of plants for every 10 pounds (5 kg) it weighs. That's 10 percent of its body weight. If you weighed 80 pounds (36 kg), you would have to eat 8 pounds (4 kg) of salad a day to keep up with a manatee!

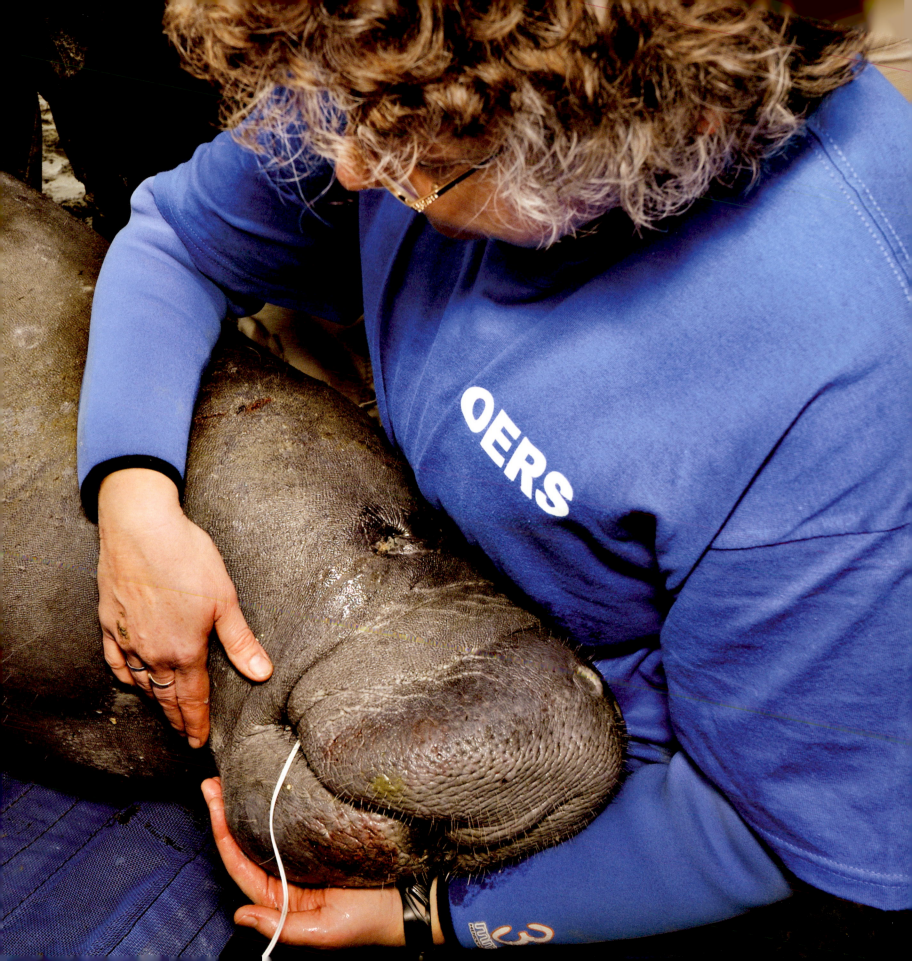

MAN & MANATEE

Even though manatees today have no natural predators, they face a number of threats to their survival. Some of these threats come from nature, but most stem from human activity.

Perhaps the greatest natural threat to manatees is red tide. Red tide is caused by types of algae that contain toxins, or poisonous substances. These algae are single-cell organisms that are always living in offshore waters in low numbers, but sometimes they multiply in what are known as "blooms." These blooms are called red tide. The toxins can make animals such as seabirds, whales, dolphins, and manatees very sick and can even kill them. An outbreak of red tide killed more than 150 manatees in 1996.

People used to hunt manatees for food and for their hides, oil, and bones. Many were killed. Today, fewer than 4,000 manatees remain in Florida. They are considered an endangered species. We now have laws to protect manatees. But manatees still face two big threats: motorboats and loss of warm-water habitat.

Since manatees move slowly and spend a lot of their time close to the surface of the water, they can get hit by speeding motorboats. Many manatees have scars on their bodies from boat propellers. Sometimes the manatee is killed or badly hurt. Scientists often tag these injured animals so they can track them and help them.

The other big threat manatees face is the loss of warm-water habitat. Some wetlands in Florida have been filled in to create more space because so many people have moved to the state. This has destroyed or harmed some of the warm-water areas that manatees flock to in cold weather.

As the population in Florida grew, more power plants were built along the coast. These power plants release warm water back into the ocean, so

Top: A manatee swims with a satellite tracking device attached to its tail. The tag comes off easily if it gets tangled up in vegetation. Bottom: Buddy Powell uses a satellite receiver to track a tagged manatee. Tracking helps scientists gather information and monitor injured or recovering animals.

In the winter, manatees gather near the warm waters of Three Sisters Springs on the Crystal River. The area is roped off to keep people and motorboats out.

HOW IS A MANATEE LIKE A MERMAID?

Ancient folktales tell of mermaids, or sirens, who sing to sailors and lure them to their deaths. People now think these were really manatees.

The name for the scientific order for manatees, Sirenia, comes from these siren tales.

In 1493, Christopher Columbus thought he saw mermaids off the coast of Hispaniola. They "rose well out of the sea" and had "the form of a human face."

Power plants warm the water to a comfortable 72°F (22°C). In winter, manatees flock to this area along the Riviera Beach Power Plant to stay warm.

they created new places for manatees to migrate to, often farther north than manatees used to go.

Today, some of these power plants are being shut down. Manatees will no longer have the warm water they need to live. Many may die as a result.

Population growth affects manatees in other ways too. To provide water for everyone, more wells are drilled. These wells take water away from the springs and rivers where manatees live. As the freshwater level drops, salt water from the ocean can move inland into the rivers. The salt can kill the freshwater plants that manatees eat. Manatees must then travel much farther downriver and into the sea to find food.

Pollution or trash in the water is another big threat to all marine life. Manatees can die from swallowing plastic bags. They can also get tangled in fishing lines.

SAVING

Florida manatees bask in the warmth of the shallow water while they recover from injury at Homosassa Springs Wildlife State Park.

THE MANATEE

Today, instead of hunting manatees, people travel from all over the world just to see them. This kind of tourism helps people appreciate manatees, and it can help teach people about the kinds of human activities that threaten manatees.

A Florida manatee swims under a school of mangrove snapper fish in the Weeki Wachee River in northwest Florida.

To help protect manatees, sanctuaries have been created. These are areas that are off-limits to people. Another thing that helps is reducing the speed limit for boats in manatee habitats.

Many groups are working to save manatees. Local

← *This manatee looks like it's waving to us!*

volunteers patrol the waterways looking for sick or injured manatees. They take them to a rehabilitation center, where the manatee is treated. After it gets better, it is released back into the wild, often with a satellite tag, so researchers can monitor it.

Most of what we know about manatees has been learned within just the last few decades. Scientists today use a variety of tools and techniques to study them. Satellite tags not only track injured manatees, they also help scientists learn about migrations and dives. Scientists sometimes view manatees from an airplane to assess habitats and population.

Along with our growing interest in conservation, perhaps the best hope for the future is the manatee's ability to adapt. Manatees have adapted from being once completely wild to living alongside people in urban areas. We humans are fortunate to have such beautiful marine animals living among us, and we are starting to appreciate them. If we continue to learn about and respect manatees and other wildlife, the future for manatees can be bright. It's up to us!

HOW YOU CAN HELP

⬇ *In some places, like Florida's Crystal River, you are allowed to swim near manatees. Generally, it's best to watch them from a safe distance.*

The best way to help manatees, like all endangered animals, is to learn about the problems facing them. Read books and magazines and visit Web sites that contain current information about manatees.

Next, take action. No matter where you live, you can make choices that protect the environment. Recycle in your home, and never throw trash on the ground, in the ocean, or in rivers. Instead of buying bottled water, which creates plastic trash that often ends up polluting our water, use a water bottle that can be refilled over and over again for years.

Talk to your family, teachers, and friends about what you've learned about manatees and other wildlife. Helping people understand wildlife conservation is one of the most important things you can do.

▬ At Web sites such as www.savethemanatee.org, you can not only learn all about manatees, but also "adopt" one for a small fee. The money is used for manatee conservation.

You can also adopt a manatee as a gift for a friend!

▬ You can help the rehabilitation and release of injured manatees, follow their movements back in the wild, or learn about other manatee research by visiting www.sea2shore.org.

▬ If you live in Florida or plan to visit the state, ask your parents to take you to see manatees in the wild. They can often be found near urban areas or major tourist attractions. If you see a manatee, obey the rules. Never chase or tease them.

▬ If you are boating in Florida, make sure that you go slow in the Manatee Speed Zones. If you accidentally hit a manatee or see a sick, injured, or dead manatee, be sure to report it by calling 1-888-404-3922.

▬ Florida residents can get manatee license plates. The money raised from the sale of these license plates goes toward manatee research.

IT'S YOUR TURN

Not everyone can come face to face with manatees in the wild. Some zoos and marine parks have manatee exhibits where you can watch them, but most of these places are in Florida. You can also see captive manatees in Ohio and California. If you can't see a manatee in person, watch videos of them. Many libraries have wildlife videos. You can find links to online videos and to manatee exhibits in the Find Out More section on page 30.

— As you watch manatees, take notes about how they move and how they interact with each other. Make some sketches of them. Carefully draw any scars you see on the animals. Manatees in the wild often have scars from being hit by boats or from other accidents. Researchers use these scars to identify individual manatees.

— Elephants are the closest land relative of the manatee. Watch elephants at a zoo, and then compare the way they look and move to the way manatees do. How does the elephant's trunk compare to the manatee's snout? Elephants have nails on their toes. Do manatees have nails? Check out the picture below!

The thick bristles on a manatee's snout help it grab food and get it into its mouth.

FACTS AT A GLANCE

⬇ *The wide, flat tail of a manatee helps it glide slowly through the water.*

Types of Manatees

There are three species of manatees: West Indian, West African, and Amazonian. The Florida manatee is a subspecies of the West Indian. Manatees belong to the scientific order Sirenia. The dugong is another type of Sirenian. It is similar in many ways to the manatee.

Size

Manatees grow 8 to 13 feet (2.4 to 4 m) in length, and they can weigh up to 1,300 pounds (600 kg). The West Indian manatee is the largest type of manatee. Female manatees are usually larger and heavier than males.

Life Span

In the wild, manatees can live 50 years or longer.

Habitat and Range

Manatees live in warm waters. They are found in both fresh-water and salt water. They inhabit shallow, slow-moving rivers, bays, canals, and coastal areas. The West Indian manatee lives in coastal areas from the southeastern United States to

Brazil. The Amazonian manatee inhabits the Amazon River in South America. The West African manatee is found along the western coast of Africa. The dugong lives in coastal areas of the Indian Ocean and the western Pacific Ocean. The majority of dugongs live near Australia.

Food

Manatees are plant eaters, or herbivores. They feed on a wide variety of plants that grow in the water and at the water's edge, including water weeds, sea grasses, and algae. Manatees spend four to eight hours a day eating, and they consume huge amounts of food. They can eat about one-tenth of their body weight in plant matter daily.

Behavior

Manatees are slow-moving, gentle animals that spend their entire lives in the water. They may travel great distances to migrate between their winter and summer feeding grounds. Manatees rarely fight each other. Because they seem as calm as cows grazing in a meadow, they

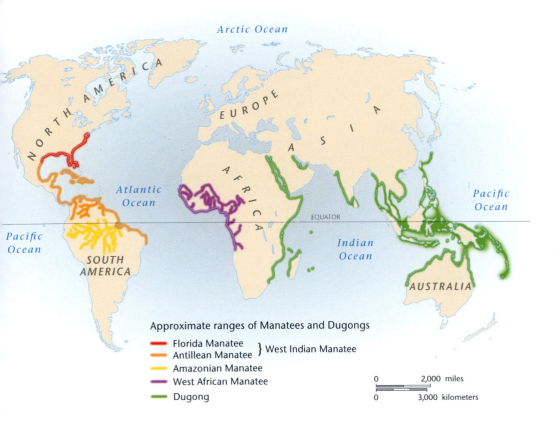

↑ *The map above shows the range of manatees and dugongs around the world.*

are sometimes called sea cows. Manatees are usually seen alone, in pairs, or in small groups of three to six. When swimming, they rise to the surface to breathe air every 3 to 4 minutes. When resting, they can go 10 minutes or so between breaths. Manatees nuzzle each other and sometimes make contact with their tails and flippers. They seem to recognize each other by the chirps, squeaks, and other noises they make.

Special Features

Long, thick bristles on the manatee's upper lip help the animal eat. These bristles are used like fingers to tear off pieces of plants and push them into the animal's mouth. Another interesting feature is its teeth. As a manatee's front teeth get worn down from grinding food, they fall out and are replaced by rear teeth that move forward. Manatees keep replacing these teeth, called marching molars, as long as they live.

Reproduction

Manatee females are pregnant for about 12 to 14 months before they give birth. They usually have only one baby, called a calf, at a time. A calf drinks its mother's milk. It begins to eat plants after a few months. Calves stay with their mothers for up to two and a half years.

Biggest Threats

The greatest human-related threats to manatees are the loss of warm-water habitat and collisions with motorboats. Because there are so few of them in the wild, Florida manatees are listed as an endangered species. All manatee species—as well as the dugong—are considered threatened, which means that they are likely to become endangered unless the problems threatening their survival improve.

GLOSSARY

Adapt: To become suited to one's surroundings. Animals can adapt to changes in the environment over many generations.

Algae: Simple plants and organisms that grow in water.

Calves: Baby manatees.

Dugong: A close relative of the manatee.

Endangered: A species with very few individuals remaining. If the number of individuals rises, the classification may change to "threatened" or "recovered." If the number falls, the species may become "extinct," meaning no individuals are left.

Graze: To feed on grasses or other plants.

Habitat: The local environment in which an animal lives.

Herbivore: A plant-eating animal.

Mermaid: A mythical sea creature with the head and upper body of a woman and the tail of a fish.

Migration: The seasonal movement of animals from one place to another.

Nurse: To feed young with milk from special glands in the mother's body.

Range: The area where an animal lives.

Snout: A long, projecting nose.

Species: A group of animals or plants that look similar, can breed with one another, and have offspring who can also breed successfully.

FIND OUT MORE

Books & Articles

Arnosky, Jim. *All About Manatees.* Scholastic, 2008.

McDonald, Mary Ann. *Manatees.* The Child's World, 2007.

Powell, James. *Manatees: Natural History & Conservation.* Voyager Press, 2002.

Reep, Roger L., and Robert K. Bonde. *The Florida Manatee: Biology and Conservation.* University Press of Florida, 2006.

Reynolds, John E., and Daniel K. Odell. *Manatees and Dugongs.* Facts On File, 1991.

Sleeper, Barbara, and Jeff Foott. *In the Company of Manatees.* Three Rivers Press, 2000.

Swinburne, Stephen R. *Saving Manatees.* Boyds Mill Press, 2006.

Web Sites

http://www.savethemanatee.org/
All about manatees and efforts to help them. Click on "Cool Manatee Stuff" for links to videos, postcards, stickers, music, games, and more.

http://www.savethemanatee.org/places.htm
A list of places where you can see manatees in the wild and in captivity.

http://animals.nationalgeographic.com/animals/mammals/manatee.html
Listen to manatee sounds and watch a video about manatee detection.

http://www.seaworld.org/animal-info/info-books/manatee/index.htm
Information about manatees.

http://fl.biology.usgs.gov/Manatees/manatees.html
Manatee research, fact sheets, and a screen saver.

http://www.sea2shore.org/
Conservation projects for manatees and other endangered water animals.

INDEX

Boldface *indicates illustrations.*

RESEARCH & PHOTOGRAPHIC NOTES

Photographers spend a lot of time thinking about equipment and technology. But I believe the most important thing a wildlife photographer can have is patience. When working with animals like manatees, a photographer must be really patient to get the best pictures. When we first see an animal, we might want to swim right in and make a picture, but if we wait, we are usually rewarded with interesting, natural behavior and therefore our photos are far better.

Underwater photographers must get close to their subjects. Wildlife photographers on land can use telephoto lenses to make pictures of animals far away. But the clarity of water is never as good as that of air, so underwater photographers must use wide-angle lenses and get close. We usually have to be no farther than five or six feet away from the animals we are photographing. Difficult, yes, but many animals will allow you into their world.

When I first began working as a photographer, I used film, but today I use digital cameras. Digital technology allows me to shoot hundreds of pictures on a single dive instead of only 36 frames with film. Digital cameras have also improved our ability to shoot when not much light is available. Many of the images in this book were made late in the day, when manatees gathered in freshwater springs. Though the water was often clear, there was very little sunlight. But with digital cameras, I could shoot at high speeds, allowing me to capture not only the animal, but its surroundings as well. Being able to see the animal within its habitat helps tell a better story.

For this book, I worked with several scientists and researchers who have studied manatees for years. Their knowledge helped me understand manatee behavior better and get better pictures. I also worked with U.S. Fish & Wildlife officers, marine veterinarians, state park officials, and eco-tour operators. If you are interested in working with manatees, you might consider one of these careers. Of course, you could also be a wildlife photographer!

FOR MY DAUGHTER CAROLINE, WHO HAS BEEN FACE TO FACE WITH MANATEES. MAY YOU ALWAYS FIND PEACE AND WONDER IN THE NATURAL WORLD.

Acknowledgments

I am deeply grateful for the help and support of the many people who have dedicated their lives to learning about and saving manatees. Especially I wish to thank Dr. James "Buddy" Powell and his wife, Maureen, and daughter Morgan for their friendship and for all the time and assistance they provided. I also wish to thank Bob Bonde and Cathy Beck of the USGS for their expertise and tremendous help. Also invaluable to my work with manatees were Holly Edwards (FWC), Andy Garrett (FWC), Scott Faulkenberg (Manatee Safaris), the staff of Homosassa Springs Wildlife State Park, and the staff of SeaWorld's manatee rehabilitation facility in Orlando.

The publisher gratefully acknowledges the assistance of Christine Kiel, K-3 curriculum and reading consultant, and Dr. James "Buddy" Powell, Executive Director of the Sea to Shore Alliance, for his assistance with the maps and review of the text.

Front cover: Face to face with a manatee. *Front flap:* A manatee comes to the surface to take a breath. *Back cover:* The underside of a manatee; author Brian Skerry in his wet suit.

Book design by David M. Seager. The body text of the book is set in ITC Century. The display text is set in Knockout and Party Noid.

Published by the National Geographic Society

John M. Fahey, Jr., *President and Chief Executive Officer*

Gilbert M. Grosvenor, *Chairman of the Board*

Tim T. Kelly, *President, Global Media Group*

John Q. Griffin, *President, Publishing*

Nina D. Hoffman, *Executive Vice President; President, Book Publishing Group*

Melina Gerosa Bellows, *Executive Vice President, Children's Publishing*

Staff for This Book

Nancy Laties Feresten, *Vice President, Editor-in-Chief of Children's Books*

Jonathan Halling, *Design Director, Children's Publishing*

Jennifer Emmett, Mary Beth Oelkers-Keegan, *Project Editors*

David M. Seager, *Art Director*

Lori Epstein, *Illustrations Editor*

M.F. Delano, *Researcher*

Carl Mehler, *Director of Maps*

Sven M. Dolling, *Map Editor*

Kate Olesin, *Editorial Assistant*

Jennifer Thornton, *Managing Editor*

Grace Hill, *Associate Managing Editor*

R. Gary Colbert, *Production Director*

Lewis R. Bassford, *Production Manager*

Rachel Faulise, Nicole Elliott, *Manufacturing Managers*

Susan Borke, *Legal and Business Affairs*

Library of Congress Cataloging-in-Publication Data

Skerry, Brian.
 Face to face with manatees / By Brian Skerry.
     p. cm.
 Includes bibliographical references and index.
 ISBN 978-1-4263-0616-7 (hardcover : alk. paper) — ISBN 978-1-4263-0617-4 (library binding : alk. paper)
 1. Manatees. 2. Manatees—Pictorial works. I. Title.
 QL737.S63S55 2010
 599.55—dc22

2009040783

Founded in 1888, the National Geographic Society is one of the largest nonprofit scientific and educational organizations in the world. It reaches more than 285 million people worldwide each month through its official journal, NATIONAL GEOGRAPHIC, and its four other magazines; the National Geographic Channel; television documentaries; radio programs; films; books; videos and DVDs; maps; and interactive media. National Geographic has funded more than 8,000 scientific research projects and supports an education program combating geographic illiteracy.

For more information, please call 1-800-NGS LINE (647-5463) or write to the following address:
National Geographic Society
1145 17th Street N.W.
Washington, D.C. 20036-4688 U.S.A.

Visit us online at www.nationalgeographic.com/books. Librarians and teachers, visit us at www.ngchildrensbooks.org. Kids and parents, visit us at kids.nationalgeographic.com.

For information about special discounts for bulk purchases, please contact National Geographic Books Special Sales: ngspecsales@ngs.org. For rights or permissions inquiries, please contact National Geographic Books Subsidiary Rights: ngbookrights@ngs.org.

Printed in China.

13/RRDS/2